HOW THE EXECUTIVE BRANCH WORKS

BY MADDIE SPALDING

Published by The Child's World®
1980 Lookout Drive • Mankato, MN 56003-1705
800-599-READ • www.childsworld.com

ACKNOWLEDGMENTS
The Child's World®: Mary Swensen, Publishing Director
Red Line Editorial: Editorial direction and production
The Design Lab: Design

Photographs ©: Alex Brandon/AP Images, cover, 2; Nagel
Photography/Shutterstock Images, 5; Zack Frank/Shutterstock
Images, 6; Shutterstock Images, 7, 12 (left), 12 (middle),
12 (right), 13, 16 (top), 16 (bottom), 20; Mark Van Scyoc/
Shutterstock Images, 8; Image © Sterling and Francine Clark Art
Institute, Williamstown, Massachusetts, USA (photo by Michael
Agee/Gilbert Stuart (American, 1755–1828), George Washington,
1796–1803. Oil on canvas, 28 15/16 x 24 1/16 in. (73.5 x 61.1
cm). Sterling and Francine Clark Art Institute, Williamstown,
Massachusetts, USA, 1955.16/Detail, 10; Pete Souza/White
House, 14; Asia Glab/Shutterstock Images, 16 (middle); Tomasz
Szymanski/Shutterstock Images, 19

ISBN 9781503809031
LCCN 2015958457

Printed in the United States of America
Mankato, MN
June, 2016
PA02309

On the cover: This seal can be seen whenever the president gives a speech.

TABLE OF CONTENTS

CHAPTER 1

WHAT IS THE EXECUTIVE BRANCH?

Think about the United States. Who is the first person who comes to mind? Most likely it is the president. The president is the most visible member of the U.S. government. You might see the president on TV giving a speech or on the news.

The role of the president is an important one. But there are many people behind the scenes. These people help the president carry out government laws. They make up the **executive** branch.

The word "executive" means someone who is in charge. An executive manages other people or groups. Members of the executive branch manage laws. They also make sure people follow the laws. The president can't do this alone. The rest of the executive branch helps.

The executive branch's work is all around you. Have you ever walked over a bridge? Workers in the Department of Transportation probably built that bridge. Have you ever

Mount Rushmore shows the faces of four U.S. presidents: (left to right) George Washington, Thomas Jefferson, Theodore Roosevelt, and Abraham Lincoln. Mount Rushmore is in South Dakota.

visited a national park? Workers in the Department of the Interior take care of the national parks. They help people enjoy nature and wildlife. Both of these departments are part of the executive branch.

More than 4 million Americans work within the executive branch. The executive branch has 15 departments. The people in charge of these departments make up the president's **cabinet**. They advise the president. But the executive branch was smaller in the late 1700s.

The National Park Service (NPS) takes care of the nation's parks, such as Yellowstone National Park. The NPS is part of the Department of the Interior.

There were only three departments. That means that there were only three members of the cabinet. But the government grew. The president needed more departments and people to help.

Some departments were created out of need. Many soldiers returned to the United States after World War I.

**The Department of Defense is headquartered
at the Pentagon in Washington, DC.**

Some had trouble going back to their lives after the war.
The United States needed better services for soldiers. The
government created the Veterans Administration (VA)
in 1930. The VA changed to the Department of Veterans
Affairs in 1989. It helps soldiers who have fought in wars
for the United States.

Terrorists attacked the United States on September 11,
2001. The country needed to be better protected. The
Department of Homeland Security was created in 2002.

The Department of
Homeland Security makes
sure the country is safe
from terrorist attacks.

It tries to stop terrorist
attacks before they happen.

The executive branch
also works with two other
branches of government.
They are the legislative branch and the judicial branch.
But the executive branch is important. It helps manage the
U.S. government.

THE DEPARTMENT OF DEFENSE

The Department of Defense
is one of the 15 departments
in the executive branch. It is
the largest government agency.
This department is in charge of
military forces. These forces help
protect the country. More than
2 million people work in this
department.

CHAPTER 2

THE PRESIDENT AND HIS ADVISERS

The 13 American colonies wanted to be free from Great Britain and King George III. So they fought in the American Revolutionary War from 1775 to 1783. The colonies won the war. Later they came to be called states. They needed a new government. So **delegates** from each state wrote the Articles of Confederation. But there were problems with the new government. Each state had its own government. The **federal** government was weak. It didn't have much power over each state's government. So delegates wrote the U.S. Constitution in 1787. The Constitution included Article II. Article II created a branch that could properly **enforce** laws. It became known as the executive branch. Article II created the role of president to lead the executive branch.

The president is the head of the executive branch. The president is elected to a four-year term. Today, each president can serve only two terms.

George Washington was the first
president of the United States.

The president leads the federal government. The president lives in the White House. The White House is also where the president's office is. The president's office is sometimes called the West Wing. The president represents the United States when meeting with leaders from other countries. It is an important role. The president faces decisions that affect the country every day.

The president has other names besides "president." One is "commander in chief." That name means the president is in charge of the United States' armed forces. Other names are "chief executive" and "chief of state."

The president has two groups of advisers. They help the president make decisions. One group is the Executive Office of the President (EOP).

The White House Chief of Staff (WHCS) oversees the EOP. This person is the president's closest adviser. The WHCS helps plan the president's schedule. The WHCS also helps the different EOP departments work together. One is the Office of the Vice President.

The vice president also advises the president. The Latin word "vice" means "in place of." The vice president acts as president if something happens to the president.

BECOMING PRESIDENT

TO BECOME PRESIDENT, THE U.S. CONSTITUTION SAYS A PERSON MUST AT LEAST:

Be 35 years old

Be born in the United States

Have lived in the United States for 14 years in a row

The vice president is also called "President of the Senate." The Senate is a part of the legislative branch. It helps decide if a **bill** becomes a law. Sometimes voting on a bill ends in a tie. The vice president makes the deciding vote.

Another important office in the EOP is the National Security Council (NSC). The NSC advises the president about other countries. It also works with the military. It comes up with ways to protect the country.

The cabinet is the president's other group of advisers. The president can **appoint** members of the cabinet. The cabinet gives the president advice on many subjects. These subjects range from farming to money.

The president's plane is called Air Force One. The president uses it to visit leaders of other countries.

The 15 heads of the executive departments make up the cabinet. The vice president is also a member of the cabinet. Most department heads have the title of "secretary." The attorney general is the only department head without this title.

The attorney general is the head of the Department of Justice. This department makes sure that laws are enforced fairly. The attorney general also advises the president about the law. Other department heads make sure that Americans get the services they need. The secretary of education is in charge of the Department of Education. This department makes sure schools have enough money for students.

**The president has meetings with advisers
in the Cabinet Room.**

The secretary of health and human services oversees the
Department of Health and Human Services. Its purpose is
to protect the health of Americans.

The secretary of state oversees the State Department.
It makes sure that U.S. citizens are safe when they travel
to other countries. The secretary of defense runs the
Department of Defense. This department works with
U.S. armed forces.

The writers of the Constitution knew that the role of the
president could have a lot of power. They wanted to make

sure the president didn't become too powerful. So they suggested a system of checks and balances among the three branches. Each branch would be mostly independent. But each would also have to depend on the others. This system would keep one branch from having more power than the others.

The president can sign bills into law and make **treaties** with other countries. The president can put out an **executive order** during times of need. Executive orders have the full force of laws. Indeed, the president has a powerful role. But the other branches help keep the president's powers in check. The president does the same for the other two branches.

Congress makes up most of the legislative branch. Congress includes the Senate and the House of Representatives. Congress writes bills. The president can sign a bill into law. But the president can also turn it down, or **veto** it. Congress can stop a president's veto. Two-thirds of Congress must vote to change the president's veto.

Congress checks the president's powers in other ways. The president can choose who is in charge of executive departments. But the Senate has to authorize the president's

CHECKS AND BALANCES

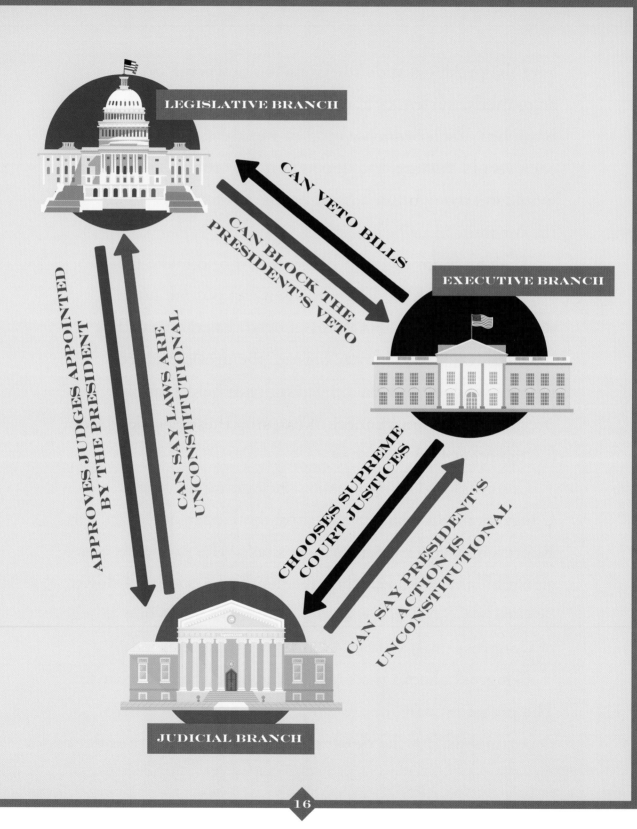

LEGISLATIVE BRANCH

EXECUTIVE BRANCH

CAN VETO BILLS

CAN BLOCK THE PRESIDENT'S VETO

APPROVES JUDGES APPOINTED BY THE PRESIDENT

CAN SAY LAWS ARE UNCONSTITUTIONAL

CHOOSES SUPREME COURT JUSTICES

CAN SAY PRESIDENT'S ACTION IS UNCONSTITUTIONAL

JUDICIAL BRANCH

choices. Checks and balances also limit the president's power to make treaties. The Senate must authorize the president's treaties in order for them to take effect. The president is the leader of the armed forces. But the president can't send the country to war if Congress doesn't allow it.

The judicial branch also keeps the president's powers in check. The Supreme Court is the main power within the judicial branch. The president can appoint judges to the Supreme Court. Then Congress must approve who the president chooses. The Supreme Court has some power over the president. It can decide if a president's decisions go against the Constitution. It can stop these decisions from taking effect.

The executive branch plays an important part in the checks and balances system. It carries out the laws that the legislative branch makes. The checks and balances system wouldn't work without the executive branch.

CHAPTER 3

INDEPENDENT AGENCIES

The 15 cabinet departments deal with big issues. But some groups handle smaller issues. They are called **independent agencies**. The president appoints the members of these agencies. Independent agencies are different from the 15 cabinet departments. Most have a board or a commission. Members of a board or a commission share power over the agency.

Railroads crossed much of the United States in the 1800s. Railroad workers built 170,000 miles (270,000 km) of tracks between 1871 and 1900. Americans could cross from one side of the country to the other. The railroad construction business was booming.

But easier travel came with a high price. Farmers thought the railroads were charging them too much to carry their goods. Some railroads had to lower their prices. The government didn't have a way to control these prices. There needed to be a way to make them fair for everyone.

The United States Postal Service makes sure citizens get their mail. The USPS is an independent agency.

The federal government took action. Lawmakers passed the Interstate Commerce Act in 1887. This act created the Interstate Commerce Commission. It was the first independent agency. It oversaw railroad prices to make sure they were fair.

The government ended the Interstate Commerce Commission in 1995. There are now other forms of transportation besides railroads. Lawmakers created the Department of Transportation in 1966. It made sure transportation was fast and safe. The Department of Transportation took over the Interstate Commerce Commission's duties.

An independent agency can have one of two jobs. Some independent agencies help carry out **policies**. Others

The Federal Reserve manages the nation's banks.

provide services. Some control a part of the U.S. economy. This includes the Federal Reserve System. The Federal Reserve manages the country's banks.

Many independent agencies offer special services. Some agencies help the government. Others help the American people. One agency is the Central Intelligence Agency (CIA). It gathers information all around the world. The CIA may find out about a plan to attack the United States. It would tell the National Security Council (NSC). The NSC is part of the Executive Office of the President. It comes up with a plan to keep the country safe.

THE CIA AND THE FBI

The CIA collects information about other countries. But it doesn't have the power to make Americans follow laws. The CIA sometimes works with the Federal Bureau of Investigation (FBI). The FBI is a group within the Department of Justice. The FBI has the power to enforce laws. The FBI can arrest people who break laws.

Lawmakers have created many other independent agencies. They created the National Aeronautics and Space Administration (NASA) in 1958. NASA studies the solar system. In 1792, Congress created the Post Office Department. The Post Office Department became an independent agency known as the United States Postal Service (USPS) in 1971. The USPS collects mail all over the country. It makes sure mail goes to the right places. Agencies like NASA and the USPS may seem very different. But they all help the government and make our lives better.

The executive branch has changed since 1787. Some cabinet departments were added and some ended. Independent agencies were created. The executive branch looks different today than it did 50 years ago. It might look different 50 years from now. But the executive branch will always have an important role in the U.S. government.

agency (AY-juhn-see) An agency is an office or department that provides a service to the public. The Department of Defense is America's largest government agency.

appoint (uh-POINT) To appoint is to choose someone for a job. The U.S. president can appoint the members of his cabinet.

bill (bil) A bill is a written plan for a new law. Lawmakers vote on bills before they are passed. The vice president has the final vote on a bill if the vote is a tie.

cabinet (KAB-in-it) A cabinet is a group of people who give advice to the head of a government. The president's cabinet is made up of 16 people.

delegates (DEL-i-gits) Delegates are people who represent a place or group. Delegates from each state planned the Constitution.

enforce (en-FORSS) To enforce is to make sure that a law or rule is obeyed. Members of the executive department enforce laws.

executive (eg-ZEK-yuh-tiv) An executive is someone who manages a group or organization. Members of the executive branch manage and enforce laws.

executive order (eg-ZEK-yuh-tiv OR-dur) An executive order is an order given by the president that has the power of a law. A president can issue an executive order in times of emergencies, such as when the United States faces a major threat.

federal (FED-ur-uhl) The federal government is the national government. The president is the head of the U.S. federal government.

independent agencies (in-di-PEN-duhnt AY-juhn-sees) Independent agencies are organizations that are separate from any of the 15 cabinet departments. Independent agencies provide services or carry out policies.

policies (POL-uh-sees) Policies are plans that people use to help them make decisions or take action. Independent agencies often help carry out U.S. government policies.

treaties (TREE-tees) Treaties are formal agreements between two or more countries. The president has the power to make treaties.

veto (VEE-toh) To veto is to prevent or delay a bill from becoming law. The president has the power to veto a bill.

TO LEARN MORE

IN THE LIBRARY

Duignan, Brian. *The Executive Branch of the Federal Government: Purpose, Process, and People.* New York: Rosen Educational Services, 2009.

Hinman, Bonnie. *The Executive Branch.* Hockessin, DE: Mitchell Lane Publishers, 2012.

Sobel, Syl. *How the U.S. Government Works.* Hauppauge, NY: Barron's, 2012.

ON THE WEB

Visit our Web site for links about
the executive branch: **childsworld.com/links**

Note to Parents, Teachers, and Librarians: We routinely verify our Web links to make sure they are safe and active sites. So encourage your readers to check them out!

INDEX

ABOUT THE AUTHOR

Maddie Spalding is an enthusiastic writer and reader. She lives in
Minneapolis, Minnesota. Her favorite part of writing is learning
about new and interesting subjects.